Cameron

by John Mackay

PUBLISHING

WRITING *to* REMEMBER

Lang**Syne**

PUBLISHING

WRITING *to* REMEMBER

Vineyard Business Centre,
Pathhead, Midlothian EH37 5XP
Tel: 01875 321 203 Fax: 01875 321 233
E-mail: info@lang-syne.co.uk
www.langsyneshop.co.uk

Design by Dorothy Meikle
Printed by Hay Nisbet Press, Glasgow
© Lang Syne Publishers Ltd 2010

ISBN 978-1-85217-035-6

Cameron

SEPT NAMES INCLUDE:
Chalmers
Clark
MacChlery
MacGillonie
MacMartin
MacPhail
MacSorley
MacUlric
Nevis
Paul
Taylor

Cameron

MOTTO:
Unite!

PLANT BADGE:
Oak

TERRITORY:
Lochaber, the area around Fort William;
Loch Eil, Loch Lochy, Glen Loy,
Glen Dessary, Glen Pean
and Loch Arkaigside

Chapter one:

The origins of the clan system

by Rennie McOwan

The original Scottish clans of the Highlands and the great families of the Lowlands and Borders were gatherings of families, relatives, allies and neighbours for mutual protection against rivals or invaders.

Scotland experienced invasion from the Vikings, the Romans and English armies from the south. The Norman invasion of what is now England also had an influence on land-holding in Scotland. Some of these invaders stayed on and in time became 'Scottish'.

The word clan derives from the Gaelic language term 'clann', meaning children, and it was first used many centuries ago as communities were formed around tribal lands in glens and mountain fastnesses.

The format of clans changed over the centuries, but at its best the chief and his family held the land on behalf of all, like trustees, and the ordinary clansmen and women believed they had a blood relationship with the founder of their clan.

There were two way duties and obligations. An inadequate chief could be deposed and replaced by someone of greater ability.

Clan people had an immense pride in race. Their relationship with the chief was like adult children to a father and they had a real dignity.

The concept of clanship is very old and a more feudal notion of authority gradually crept in.

Pictland, for instance, was divided into seven principalities ruled by feudal leaders who were the strongest and most charismatic leaders of their particular groups.

By the sixth century the 'British' kingdoms of Strathclyde, Lothian and Celtic Dalriada (Argyll) had emerged and Scotland, as one nation, began to take shape in the time of King Kenneth MacAlpin.

Some chiefs claimed descent from

ancient kings which may not have been accurate in every case.

By the twelfth and thirteenth centuries the clans and families were more strongly brought under the central control of Scottish monarchs.

Lands were awarded and administered more and more under royal favour, yet the power of the area clan chiefs was still very great.

The long wars to ensure Scotland's independence against the expansionist ideas of English monarchs extended the influence of some clans and reduced the lands of others.

Those who supported Scotland's greatest king, Robert the Bruce, were awarded the territories of the families who had opposed his claim to the Scottish throne.

In the Scottish Borders country - the notorious Debatable Lands - the great families built up a ferocious reputation for providing warlike men accustomed to raiding into England and occasionally fighting one another.

Chiefs had the power to dispense justice

and to confiscate lands and clan warfare produced a society where martial virtues - courage, hardiness, tenacity - were greatly admired.

Gradually the relationship between the clans and the Crown became strained as Scottish monarchs became more orientated to life in the Lowlands and, on occasion, towards England.

The Highland clans spoke a different language, Gaelic, whereas the language of Lowland Scotland and the court was Scots and in more modern times, English.

Highlanders dressed differently, had different customs, and their wild mountain land sometimes seemed almost foreign to people living in the Lowlands.

It must be emphasised that Gaelic culture was very rich and story-telling, poetry, piping, the clarsach (harp) and other music all flourished and were greatly respected.

Highland culture was different from other parts of Scotland but it was not inferior or less sophisticated.

Central Government, whether in London

*Clan warfare produced a society where courage
and tenacity were greatly admired*

or Edinburgh, sometimes saw the Gaelic clans as a challenge to their authority and some sent expeditions into the Highlands and west to crush the power of the Lords of the Isles.

Nevertheless, when the eighteenth century Jacobite Risings came along the cause of the Stuarts was mainly supported by Highland clans.

The word Jacobite comes from the Latin for James - Jacobus. The Jacobites wanted to restore the exiled Stuarts to the throne of Britain.

The monarchies of Scotland and England became one in 1603 when King James VI of Scotland (1st of England) gained the English throne after Queen Elizabeth died.

The Union of Parliaments of Scotland and England, the Treaty of Union, took place in 1707.

Some Highland clans, of course, and Lowland families opposed the Jacobites and supported the incoming Hanoverians.

After the Jacobite cause finally went down at Culloden in 1746 a kind of ethnic cleansing took place. The power of the chiefs was curtailed. Tartan and the pipes were banned in law.

Many emigrated, some because they wanted to, some because they were evicted by force. In addition, many Highlanders left for the cities of the south to seek work.

Many of the clan lands became home to sheep and deer shooting estates.

But the warlike traditions of the clans and the great Lowland and Border families lived on, with their descendants fighting bravely for freedom in two world wars.

Remember the men from whence you came, says the Gaelic proverb, and to that could be added the role of many heroic women.

The spirit of the clan, of having roots, whether Highland or Lowland, means much to thousands of people.

Chapter two:

A dynasty is born

In the autumn of 1745, with Scotland in the grip of the Second Jacobite Rebellion, moonlight cast a deep shadow along the east facing wall separating Edinburgh and the burgh of the Canongate; and in the gloom moved a deeper shadow, soft-footed – a detachment of Prince Charlie's Highlanders led by Cameron of Lochiel.

The clansmen moved up the wall until

their forefront reached the Canongate Port – a gateway for exit or entrance to the town. A member of the Town Guard and a gamekeeper were the only two at the Port, unaware of the presence of the warrior force.

At that moment there was a call from the Edinburgh side of the wall to open the gate and let a coach through into the Canongate. On this being done, and to the Town Guard's considerable surprise, his musket was snatched from him by a figure springing from the shadows – Cameron of Lochiel himself, followed by the Highland men who, with Gaelic yells of triumph, marched into the deserted High Street with broadswords drawn, banners flying and their pipers playing 'We'll awa to Shirramuir and haud the Whigs in order'.

It had been a bloodless victory. The gunpowder brought to blow up the Canongate Port was not required. The only inhabitants to be seen in the now early dawn light were those peering bleary-eyed from the windows of the many storied dwellings.

Sentries were posted to the other ports

around the town wall. Edinburgh had surrendered to the wild Highlanders but not its castle.

Meantime, the Prince and his army was approaching the Holyrood district by the Burghmuir and the Royal Park under Arthur's Seat.

With such happenings then and in its immediate future, it could be said that the age-old clan system was approaching its grand finale with Donald Cameron, the 'General Lochiel', as a notable example of the Highland Chief of Scotland's heroic and sometimes savage past.

As with many other clans, it is not recorded in history, in this instance the 14th century, that the Cameron clan begin to take initial form. A member of the Lochiel family married into one named 'Cambron', descendants of a warrior chieftain, who was a signatory of the Declaration of Independence for Scotland at Arbroath in 1320. And by early in the 15th century one Donald Dubh ('the dark haired') had become one of the first of the chiefs of Lochaber whose son was designated 'Captain of Clan Cameron'.

The lands of Lochaber which included the

Ben Nevis massif were long disputed over by the Camerons and the Mackintoshes though they did join forces to fight for King James I in his campaigns against the Lords of the Isles.

As reward for their services both clans were given Royal charters to lawfully hold lands in Lochaber. These did nothing to calm the feud which continued through succeeding reigns to when Donald's grandson Ewen, the 13th chief, fought at the battle of Flodden where James IV was killed.

In James V's reign Ewen was the first of the Cameron chiefs to add 'of Lochiel' to his title. Apart from the Mackintoshes, the Camerons had to contend with the Gordons on one side and the Campbells on the other – often a question of finding good grazing, fertile soil and access to fishing. Allan, the 16th chief, is noted for keeping the other menace, the Mackintoshes, successfully at bay.

His successor Ewen had the dubious distinction of killing an Englishman in battle by biting his opponent's throat.

Just south of the Killiecrankie Pass the

Cameronian regiment, raised the year after William came to the English throne in 1688, were sent to garrison Dunkeld from the Highland menace to the north and eventually house to house fighting was the order of the day soon after the rival clansmen appeared. When the Cameronians had about exhausted their supply of ammunition and while the fight went on, a detachment was sent to strip lead from the roof of the Marquis of Atholl's house to make crude but effective bullets.

The five thousand Highlanders, against 1200 Cameronians, ignorant of the strength of the opposition, decided it was not worth continuing the fight and in the tradition of raiding forces, retired from the scene, to fight another day.

At Killiecrankie Chief Ewen had fought his last battle. An eyewitness said, "It was long remembered in Lochaber that Lochiel took off what was possibly the only pair of shoes in his clan and charged barefoot at the head of his men!"

Ewen, knowing a good, reliable man when he saw one, made over his estate to his grandson Donald, the 'Gentle Lochiel' (later the 19th chief) while Ewen's eldest son, John, led the clan out on the 1715 Rising but ended as an exile never to see Lochaber again.

Donald, a notable figure in the '45, led his clan, among the first to join the Prince. He was no savage Highland chief spoiling for a fight. His estate was, or would have been, his main concern – his avenue of beeches are still there by the River Arkaig partly planted in their intended form but left incomplete on the arrival of the Prince.

Lochiel sacrificed all for his belief in the Jacobite cause; but some hindsight shows clearly how much better he would have been attending to estate matters – a worthy leader of his people in his civilized ways. His brothers were of similar nature – Alexander, a priest, and Archibald, a doctor.

Not only were the Jacobite Camerons instrumental in the taking of Edinburgh, as has already been recounted, but they were also in the vanguard of repeated, vain attempts to take the castle which were beaten back by cannon fire.

Chapter three:

Diaries from the '45

Here are some excerpts taken from diaries and memoirs written around the time of the '45.

First, notes made by Alexander Carlyle, son of the minister of Prestonpans Kirk. He had gone to visit a friend, Col. Gardener of the Dragoons, following a previous encounter with the opposition and records this talk with the colonel: "He received me with kindness and invited me to dine with him at two o'clock. I began to ask him if he was not now quite satisfied with the junction of the Foot with the dragoons, and confident that they would give account of the rebels? Said he (referring to that previous encounter): "A foul flight, Sandie, and they have not recovered from their panic; and I tell you in confidence that I have not above ten men in my regiment whom I am certain will follow me. But we must give them battle now, and God's will be done!"

Carlyle watched the Battle of Prestonpans:

"Even at that time, which could be no more than ten or fifteen minutes after firing the first cannon, the whole prospect was filled with runaways and Highlanders pursuing them. Many were still trying to reach the town in hopes of escaping…"

Later, after the battle, Carlyle visits the site of the Highland victory "on an errand of humanity" and had the opportunity of seeing the Highlanders close-up: "In general they were of low stature and dirty and of a contemptible appearance. The officers with whom I mixed were gentlemen-like and very civil to me. I was conducted to Lochiel who was polished and gentle and who ordered a soldier to make all the inquiry he could about the medicine chests of the

Dragoons. After an hour's search, we returned without finding any of them".

At the beginning of the Jacobite campaign the Bishops of Ross and Caithness, on Prince Charlie's arrival in Scotland, wrote:

"When they landed in Eriska they could not find a grain of meal or one inch of bread. But they caught some flounders, which they roasted upon some bare coals in a mean, low hut they had gone into near the shore, and Duncan Cameron stood to cook. The Prince sat at the cheek of the ingle and laughed heartily at Duncan's cooking."

After the close of the campaign, another diary, written by Donald MacPherson, younger brother of Cluny MacPherson who, with Cameron of Lochiel had been wounded at Culloden recalls:

"Lochiel tho' lame made the best of his way to meet his Royal Highness. However, such was his Royal Highness' circumspection that when the other would have kneeled at his coming up to him he said, 'Oh no, my dear Lochiel!', clapping him on the shoulder, 'You don't know who may be looking from the tops of yonder hills and if they see any such motions they'll immediately conclude that I am here.' Lochiel then ushered him into his habitation. Upon his entry he took a hearty dram and when there was some collops dress'd with butter for him in a large saucepan that Lochiel and Cluny carried always about with 'em, which was all the fire vessels they had, he ate heartily and said with a cheerful and very lively countenance, 'Now, gentlemen, I live like a Prince!' tho' at the same time he was no otherwise served than by eating his collops out of a saucepan, only that he had a silver spoon."

After further adventures Lochiel contrived to get to France where he remained in exile until his death in 1748 – his estates forfeited, the ancestral home Achnacarry and the clan houses burned to the ground.

Lochiels's brothers, the doctor and the priest, were betrayed to the Government and both were executed.

Alexander Cameron faces the hangman's noose.

Chapter four:

More great clansmen

When Bonnie Prince Charlie arrived at Glenfinnan and started the '45 Jacobite Rebellion, young Jenny Cameron was amongst those who hoped to catch a glimpse of the great man.

Within days the Government propaganda machine was spreading rumours that she was the Pretender's lover, in order to discredit him. The Whig publicity machine swung into action, including cartoons and pamphlets, and word was put round while the campaign was in progress that the Prince was being accompanied by his mistress – Miss Jenny Cameron. This smear was never especially effective but the scandal story was given fresh impetus when, by coincidence, another Jenny Cameron, a milliner in Edinburgh, was imprisoned for a brief period after the Rising was over, as she was suspected of being the other Jenny and therefore a potential menace to society

Raising the Standard at Glenfinnan.

in the event of any further Jacobite attempt against authority. She was released after mistaken identity was admitted by the Edinburgh authorities. Resuming her business of selling hats, she found that her customers greatly increased in number. Talk would get round to the Prince… Jenny would possibly give a secret smile…it was all good for trade anyhow.

The London Government banned the wearing of the kilt and tartan.

Part of the Abolition and Proscription of Highland Dress Act read:

"No man or boy within that part of Great Britain called Scotland, other than such as shall be employed as officers and soldiers in His Majesty's forces, shall, on any pretext whatever, wear or put on the clothes commonly called Highland clothes."

The act was repealed in 1782 and the Queen's Own Cameron Highlanders were raised in 1793 as the Cameronian Volunteers. A year later they were titled the Cameron Highlanders and not until 1873 did they become "The Queen's Own".

Alan Cameron of Erracht at his own expense raised the Cameron Highlanders and was appointed their Lieutenant-Colonel Commandant. The regiment fought throughout the Peninsular War. After Alan had been promoted Brigade Commander, his eldest son took over the command and was killed in action. The Duke of Wellington later paid this glowing tribute: "He fell at the head of your regiment in an action in which, if possible, the British troops surpassed anything they had ever done before."

The regiment fought in all the major campaigns from Waterloo to the war in South Africa in Victorian times and were among the first batallions to land in France with the British Expeditionary Force in World War One (during which the regiment was awarded four Victoria Crosses).

Another regiment, The Cameronians (Scottish Rifles), were named after Richard Cameron. Originally 'an elder was appointed to each company and every man carried a Bible in his kit'.

A curious link with the French Revolution

caused an eventual joining of the Cameronians with Graham of Balgowan's 'Greybreeks' – the Perthshire Volunteers (Light Infantry).

Thomas Graham, related to the Duke of Montrose, married Mary Shaw, daughter of the 9th Baron Cathcart who had been an Ambassador to the Court in Russia. Mary was 17 at the time, Graham 10 years her senior. Graham arranged that Gainsborough should paint her portrait which was completed when she was 18 and this master-work can be seen in the National Gallery of Scotland in Edinburgh. Sadly, Mary some years later contracted tuberculosis and in an attempt to bring her back to better health they had left their Perthshire home to seek a kinder climate in the south of France which they visited twice – the last in 1792 where near Nice as they were coasting along the Mediterranean, the young wife died.

The journey home began, first heading for Bordeaux by canal where they were stopped by drunken terrorists. The French Revolution was just developing and the revolutionaries insisted, suspecting only smuggled goods inside, that the coffin be opened. The enraged husband was held back by the gang while the lid was forced up – the sight met must surely have sobered all in such a criminal act.

A ship was boarded on the west coast of France and so, back to Scotland. This interlude ends with Thomas Graham, once a placid, country squire, nursing such hatred of the French that he sold part of his estate and raised the Balgowan 'Greybreeks' who linked with the Cameronians in 1794. Graham at one time became second-in-command to the Duke of Wellington.

The Cameronians were disbanded in 1968 when the Government reduced army numbers. Previously, in 1961 the Queen's Own Cameron Highlanders had been amalgamated with the Seaforth Highlanders to become The Queen's Own Highlanders.

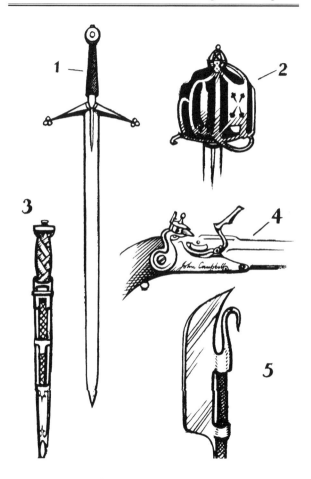

Highland weapons

1)   The claymore or two-handed sword
      (fifteenth or early sixteenth century)

2)   Basket hilt of broadsword
      made in Stirling, 1716

3)   Highland dirk
      (eighteenth century)

4)   Steel pistol *(detail)* made in Doune

5)   Head of Lochaber Axe as carried
      in the '45 and earlier